T0149752

WHEN I'M OLD AND WISE

Collected Poems

Henry T. Contreras

authorHOUSE®

AuthorHouse™
1663 Liberty Drive
Bloomington, IN 47403
www.authorhouse.com
Phone: 1 (800) 839-8640

Published by AuthorHouse 06/08/2018

ISBN: 978-1-5462-4634-3 (sc)
ISBN: 978-1-5462-4633-6 (e)

Library of Congress Control Number: 2018906850

Print information available on the last page.

CONTENTS

There are many styles of poetry
reflecting a world of poets.
It is a language painted on canvas that
can be seen even in the night.
There's something profoundly beautiful about that.

TOUCHING AUTUMN

Leaves of a match touching autumn.

He looked like a sailor standing there.
With a turtle neck and careless hair.
Gathering piles of fall.

The delayed cracking of branches from the silence of breaking.

I smelt the burning oak as grey rivers flow.

The orange embers fly.
Reminiscent of the harvest trees.

I turn to sudden gust that blow and stay.
In autumns fire where warmth calls.

It's shadow cold and lingers.
Pressing and blowing breath in my fingers.

I forgot winter is near, but it remembered.

DON'T LET TIME WALK
IN THE NIGHT

Don't let time walk away into the night.

Then will only seasons remind us of moments when we said hello.

And spring the laughter we so easily showed.

And fall when we realized something was wrong.

And winter when it was all gone.

Stay with here, all summer long.

SINGING

I ran barefooted in the cold night air.
The winter grass stinging like bees.

But I sang smiling.
Looking up to the moon I sang smiling.
It shined bright it woke my shadow by my side.
We played in the night the way imaginary friends come to life.

I returned home, she wasn't there.
I know soon too I must go.

The grass has grown with time gone by.
I buried her song when she closed her eyes.
I could still feel the moon watching over me at night.

THE OWLS FLIGHT

Keeper of the night.
I hear your cries.

The hollow breaks of wings in flight.
Watch over her endless sky.

Fly,
Noble knight.

Rise,
Keeper of the night.

Perched high amongst the sycamore trees.
I hear you when I close my eyes.
Somewhere near keeping guard.

ALPHABET STREETS

The sun lit the way from street named after trees and states.
To grandma's arms on streets named after alphabets.

I was seven and she died when I was nine, on December
twenty fifth.
My aunt took me and worked all the time, so we barely
said hello.

Mom died at forty seven,
and dad shortly after,
on state streets that I remember.

I graduated in eighty six and travelled states
that were on street signs that I remembered.

I returned from roads overgrown with bridges of trees
to open arms of my aunt living on alphabet streets.

We both were grown.
Now I exist and she is sick.
Making things right on street named after alphabets.

NORTH DAKOTA
STORMY SKIES

The first cloud had much to say.
It's dark now please make way.
Getting rid of all its rays.
To the loud percussions that has started to play.
A kaleidoscope of lights and shimmer falls from the sky.
To a crescendo which makes the air fly.

UNTIL HELLO

Some other time, some other place.
You must of known my name.

Although I must go.
I hold onto hello.

If you need me don't call.
I'll return early next fall.

MILES OF TAR AND STARS

The city grew smaller as I drove away.
The light's dimmer.

Miles of black tar and stars until
my eyes reached the other side.

Rushed, awaken across miles of fields between town to town.
The quietness resembling loneliness.

It's where I took my first breath and saw the road before me.

THE WIND FALLING FROM THE NORTH

I spread my arms from west to east,
in northern night streams I am free.

Following hollow without sight.
Gypsies of the cold night taking sight,
black birds stare.

There's something about the wind that feels hollow.

Bending and cutting trees sing.
Freeing the night in its flight.
All around hidden in sight.

I feel it push and tug again.
It is heading west along the river bed.

I WAS LATE FOR DINNER

I hurried home when I heard the news.
I'm sorry I was late.

I could smell cookies in the empty cookie jar.
I could see the white sheets pinned down wanting to be free.
Looking out of the kitchen window.

I'm not distracted but it's starting to rain.
I'll help you bring the laundry in.

I know its heavy,
I'll hold on one side and help you in.

I'm sorry I'm late for dinner.

The storm will pass and night will come.
So will talk when the conversation has begun.

*The only way to get through to him was
to write yourself into his story.*

YOUR HOME GOT STUCK
IN MY SPIDER WEB

Your home got stuck in my spider web,
but you arrived on time.

So I dangled my feet over every thought you shared.
I heard your silence and knew there was something there.
I saw you smile, secrets not even you knew waiting to be
spared.

What part do you think I don't understand?
When every part of me had to be put back together again.
It's late and we have stumbled over our words to long.

Look there's a feather at your side.
Tear open your chest and let the birds fly with the sky.

RAISE YOU CHALICE

Raise your chalice and wear paper hats.
I'll be living in my favorite Photograph.

They are waiting.
So I'll wait too.

Until I close my eyes.

Look for a sign when birds fly.
Then you'll know I have arrived.

I HEAR A NOISE

I hear a noise in your heart.
Let your worries drown by the sunset near the shore.
Feel the wind stand with you in the sun.
The sky is yours and the new day that has begun.

I AM RETURNING HOME

I am returning home piece by piece,
by the hands that created me.

Until the last grains of earth falls through an hour glass.

Tomorrow's landscape will change,
But the heart will always stay.

I tried to recreate myself only to find myself.

PASSERBY

I am a passerby.
I saw the trash in alley ways.

I walked home in the rain.
Just the same in the sun.

There's a song escaping someone's home.
Someone's child must be learning to play.

I placed my head down when I heard crying from a window. .
I smiled when I heard laughing.

I stopped in front of a coffee shop.
The news showed towers falling in down.
I sat on the curb when I heard how many had fallen.

I stopped and looked at the beautiful night.
A plane was flying by.

I gave a homeless man a dollar.
We talked for an hour.
He smiled and said God is good.

I got home and called a friend.
I told him I was blessed.

I am a passerby.
A flash in a thunderstorm.

THE FIRE-STORM

The sleeping valley in yellow.
The hills are on fire.

The flames are climbing high.
They're burning the sky.

The winds have arrived
so has darkness.

Go cross the dry river beds latched in stone.

Let them know to leave their homes.

The glow is not the sun.

The heat is angry.
It is hungry.

I see smoke.
The morning is coming.

The cathedrals of forest have fallen so has the town.

My face stained in ash of all that is gone.
So were my dreams in the day's to come.

I SHINE

I shine.
I go dark.
I dance on saturns rings.
I love. I lost.
I will always be,
Eternity's synchrony.

OUTWALK THE LIGHT

I outwalked the light to capture thoughts in the night.
Walking farther than city blocks.

Honeysuckles slept as I walked by,
smelling soft as the breeze.

Silence! the darkness called-out,
hearing chatter escape my mind and onto the streets.

My eyes open.
Mountains outlined by the moon.

A cat following me.
A star flying free.

My flesh growing on my bones.
Each step timed with beats in my chest as I manifest.
I drop my arms to the night who welcomed me.

I HIT THE GROUND

Pray for me on the way down.
Lift me up when I hit the ground.

Wipe the floor off my knees.

Rise with me.
Don't look down.

Rise again like the sun.

WHO ARE WE TO SAY

Who are we to say it can't be.
The saddest thing to believe is someone is listening.

We are architects and masons laying down stones.

We have a dream that wants to mate with destiny.

Release them from your ribs and trenches.

Let them bud like roses once frozen.

From Gods hand where they were meant to be free.

We have a dream that wants to mate with destiny.

IF I DIDN'T BARE WITNESS

If I didn't bare witness from the shadows.

I wouldn't have seen a firefly at sunset.

I wouldn't have seen the northern lights dance at night.

I wouldn't have stayed awake through darkness to watch the sunrise.

I wouldn't have seen the seasons change and rain.

MY CLOCK DIED

My clock died as it looked my way.
Whispering in its last few breaths.

Life is measured by moments not time.

I could hear It's heart beat in its chest.
Tick- tock, tick, tock, tick.

The clock still sits on my desk.
Reminding me of moments and time.

THE RAIN DROP SAILS

The rain drops sailed down my brow.
Into the arms of the sea it fell.

I am home where I belong.
The sun beating through red clouds.

As I manage tempered sails.
Into the horizon and swells.

I am heading home too where I belong,
tomorrow I'll sail this is not farewell.

We fall in love with an ideal of what love is until it finds us.

THE SMELL OF RAIN

I was a dreamer in your reality.
Standing in the sun with the smell of rain in the air.
We drove in silence to catch a plane.
A storm rising in my eyes.
So I didn't turn to say goodbye.

THE SEASON OF THE HUMMINGBIRD

The season of spring had two faces.

The flowers bloomed and the fire turned to dirt.

The sun rose and the ice burned.

The ground drowned from the flooded sky.

You said hello and said goodbye.

And the hummingbird gave birth above the earth....

LOVE AND EPIC NOVELS

Our love wasn't an epic novel, but a poem I'm glad I wrote.

It didn't go down as a one of the romance classics,
but just the same it was full of love.

It didn't last the test of time,
but forever stayed in my heart and mind.

It was great seeing you again even if it was only in my dreams.

MY FRIEND MY HEART

I got the news you went away.

I felt my knees hit the ground.

I felt helpless because I couldn't call.

You see,

When we said goodbye, I didn't know I would never see you again.

I thought our goodbye meant the sun would break through the foggy days.

That morning would come despite the night.

That the clouds would dissipate despite the rain.

When we talked, we just needed time.

My love never changed,
but we crossed a line and needed time.

How does the heart continually break.
Like a frozen lake late in spring.

Because,

I really thought I'd see you again.

SPLIT THE NIGHT

I split the night when I walk and it was white.

Saline stains the same as bleach.

Photograph's frozen in time I can't break the ice.

There's a lump in my throat.

I saw lights flicker and knew it was you.

I faintly smelled your perfume from the corner of my eyes.

I forgot the name but remember the smell of honeydew.

The silence grey.
Wait!

Remember we would sit at night watching stars on the shore.
Wait!

Before you go, please know, I do you love you.
Although there is a lump in my throat.

BEFORE I WENT AWAY

I heard the sound of rain before I went away.
My body lifeless in the night where I lay.

As I roam shrouded roads along the way.
Seeing reflections of other days.

Until I'm home where I lay.

SOME OTHER TIME

Who were we before we were born.
Were we huddled watching lightning in a thunder storm.

Were we soldiers drunk on the sand.
You knew my story when you turned to glance.

I must of known you, was it by chance,
as we crossed each other's paths.

Our words spoken in riddles and rhymes.
I must of known you some other time.

THE GREY BETWEEN

The grey between joy and sorrow.

Is where poems are written,
walking with horns and drums.

The sun will rise.
Darkness will fall.

So I say it's an overcast day.

Sunburned and alive.
Watching the skies for words not born.

RAISE YOU CHALICE

Raise your chalice and wear paper hats.
I'll be living in my favorite Photograph.

They are waiting.
So I'll wait too.
Until I close my eyes.

Look for a sign when birds fly.
Then you'll know I have arrived.

LIFE MOVING AT THE SPEED OF LIGHT

I see life moving slowly at the speed of light.
Images blurred as they walk on by.

Speaking to the wind who steals their words.
It's all muffled sounds until I speak.

Listen to me. Listen to me I say. Stop.
Look around. Stop. Look around I say.

MATHEW 12/98.

My throat drowned in emotion.
Human kindness was over whelming.

Their hatred cheered.
Their palms did swear.
Their anger shared.

Angeles sang amazing grace.
They spat in your face.

Human kindness was overwhelming.

Confessions told despite the sin.
They built a wall so their words didn't escape.
Our hands heard across our face.

Human kindness was overwhelming.

Many prayed but for who in the end.

Human kindness was overwhelming.
Will someone please let them in.

WE WILL BUILD A SWING

We will gather friends,
and build a swing.

With blueprints made in the sand.

We will use the strongest tree and forest for everyone.

We will swing real high until we realize.
It's our yard, from land to land and every side.

When I'm old and wise.
I'll look back at every
photograph breathing on my wall.
I'll remember every curve of love.
Say hello to goodbyes.
I will laugh.
I will cry.
And I will know I have travelled
on every vein from the heart.

To my dearest aunt Celia Mascorro.
Thank you for always being there when my parents
passed and for believing in me when the heart was
inconsolable and uncontrolled. I love you and I hope
to inherit half the strength and love you have given.

To Richard, Vincent and Yvonne.
I am so proud of you and love you with
all my heart my brothers and sister.

To Gloria Davila.
Keep shining the way you do. Everything
you do has never gone unnoticed.

To Lisa Hernandez and Robert Hernandez.
I will always believe in you.

To Amber Mayes.
You will always be my touch stone
and I'm glad you're here.

To Tony Clubb, Mark McMaster, Tim
Houston and Abbie Sheppherd.
Life is good with lifetime friends.

To my dearest friend Christene Lentz.
Your love and friendship has led the way. Who's dreams
we shared by the shore. Rest in peace my dear friend.
When I look at stars, I know your there.

To Joyce Lentz.
Thank you for your support and believing in me.
It has always been a big part of my heart and who
helped develop me to be the best man I can be.
Thank you helping me with my
homework when I was late.

To Sloan Warner.
Thank you for believing in dreams and for being you.

To Alex Alico.
Because you believed in me you motivated me.

To my writer family.
Amy, Soulla, Melissa, Susie, Aaron, Tim and Jackie
We spoke about everything thing. Your
talents inspired me to write.
Your continuous support made things real.

To my dearest family and friends.
This book is for you.

Printed in the United States
By Bookmasters